Discovering Science

YO-BEK-325

Air, Water and Weather

Michael Pollard

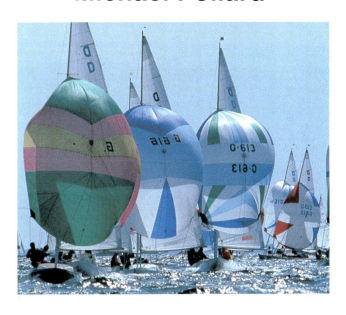

Facts On File Publications
New York, New York ● Oxford, England

WITHDRAWN
HIEBERT LIBRARY
FRESNO PACIFIC UNIV
FRESNO, CA 93702

Research Library
AIMS Education Foundation
Fresno, CA 93747-8120

Contents

NOTE TO THE READER: while you are reading this book you will notice that certain words appear in **bold type**. This is to indicate a word listed in the Glossary on page 45. This glossary gives brief explanations of words which may be new to you.

Acknowlegements

The Publishers wish to thank the following organizations for their invaluable assistance in the preparation of this book.

Airship Industries
Central Electricity Generating Board

Photographic credits

t = top b = bottom l = left r = right c = center

5 Mike Potts/Seaphot; 6/7, 11 ZEFA; 13 NHPA; 14 ZEFA; 15 Airship Industries; 16l Warren Williams/Seaphot; 16r Brian Coope/Seaphot; 18/19 ZEFA; 20 Ed Lawrenson; 21, 23l ZEFA; 23r Central Electricity Generating Board; 26, 27 ZEFA; 34 The Hutchison Library; 35, 36, 40 ZEFA; 41 Dundee University; 42 Peter Stevenson/Seaphot; 44 ZEFA

Illustrations by David Anstey, George Fryer/Linden Artists; Sallie Alane Reason; Brian Watson/Linden Artists

Discovering Science/Air, Water and Weather

Copyright © BLA Publishing Limited 1987

First published in the United States of America by Facts on File, Inc. 460 Park Avenue South, New York, New York 10016.

All rights reserved. No part of this book may be reproduced or utilized in any form or by any means, electronic or mechanical, including photocopying, recording or by any information storage and retrieval systems, without permission in writing from the Publisher.

Library of Congress Catalog Card Number:
87-80101

Designed and produced by BLA Publishing Limited, East Grinstead, Sussex, England.

A member of the **Ling Kee Group**
LONDON · HONG KONG · TAIPEI · SINGAPORE · NEW YORK

Printed in Italy by New Interlitho

10 9 8 7 6 5 4 3 2 1

Air, water and weather

The Earth is a **planet** which is able to support life. It has air which animals and plants can breathe. We could not stay alive for more than a few minutes without air. The Earth also has water. All living things need water. Without water, we would die in a few days.

The climate of the Earth

Living things also need heat. The Sun is just the right distance from the Earth. Because of this, the Earth's **climate** is neither too hot nor too cold for plant and animal life.

The Earth's water and air are moving all the time. The heat of the Sun warms the water of the oceans. They give off clouds of **water vapor**. These clouds are blown by the winds and become cool. Then the water vapor turns into rain or snow. Rain and snow drain into rivers which flow back into the oceans. No water is lost.

Air also moves from place to place, giving us winds. The flow of water and air, and the heat of the Sun, together give the Earth its weather. The weather changes all the time.

What is air?

You cannot see air. You cannot smell it or hear it. Yet it is around you all the time. Without it, you could not live.

You can feel air if you wave your hand quickly in front of your face. Your hand pushes the air and makes a small wind. If you ride fast on a bicycle you can feel the air rushing into your face. On a very windy day the flow of air can be so strong that it can blow you over.

What is air made of?

Everything on the Earth is a **solid**, a **liquid** or a **gas**. Hard things like steel or rock are solids. Things that flow like water or oil are liquids. Most gases cannot be seen.

The air we breathe is a mixture of different gases. One of these is **oxygen**. Animals and plants need oxygen to stay alive.

Can air be squashed?

If you try to pour water from a full bottle into a smaller, empty bottle, some of the water will be left over. You cannot squash a liquid into a smaller space, however hard you try.

Gases work in a different way than liquids. Air spreads out thinly to fill all the space around us. When a gas is spread out thinly, it has a low **pressure**.

Lighter than air

If you fill a balloon with air and let it go, it will float to the ground. Some gases are lighter than air. A balloon filled with **hydrogen** or **helium** will easily float up into the air. Airships filled with helium can carry people and freight. They float above the ground and have engines to drive them forward.

▲ These yachts have plenty of wind to help them. Wind is just moving air.

When it is squashed into a smaller space, it has a high pressure.

We can pump air into a small space, so that it is at high pressure. We do this when we blow up a balloon, a tire or a football. If a balloon bursts, it makes a bang. This is because the air at high pressure all rushes out at once.

7

Warming air

When we breathe in air, it takes in warmth from our bodies. The air we breathe out is warm. This is why people often blow on their hands to warm them on a cold day. Perhaps you have sometimes blown into your gloves to make them warm before putting them on.

In cold weather, we make our houses warm by heating the air inside them. In hot weather, some homes are kept cool by air-conditioning. This cools the air inside the rooms of a house.

Expansion of air

When air is warmed it takes up more space. This is called **expansion**. Here is an experiment. It shows you that warm air expands. You will need a piece of soap and a bottle made of glass that is not too thick.

Make some lather with the soap and put a film of lather across the neck of the bottle. Then warm the bottle with your hands. As the air in the bottle warms up, it expands and needs more room. This expanding air pushes up the film of lather to make a bubble.

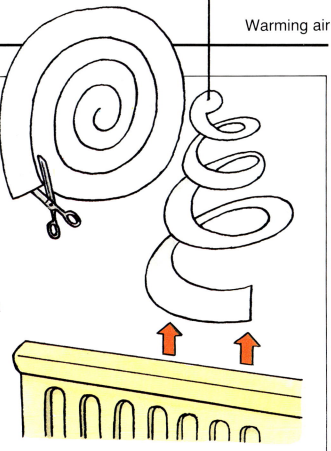

Hot air rises

As air warms up, it rises. When a radiator is turned on, warm air rises from it and spreads around the room. This movement of warm air is called **convection**. Cold air passes near the bottom of the radiator. It rises as it warms up.

You can see how warm air rises. Make a spiral mobile like the one in the picture. Use stiff paper. When you have cut out the spiral, hang it on a thread over a radiator. Soon, it will begin to turn as the warm air reaches the under side of the paper. The warm air provides a **force** which makes the mobile turn.

Hot air cooling

There is always some dampness or **moisture** in the air. At home, some of it comes from your breath. It also comes from the steam given off in cooking. Warm air takes up the moisture in tiny drops. Moist, warm air is called water vapor.

Cold air cannot hold as much moisture as warm air can. When warm air meets a cold surface, it loses some of its moisture. This happens if you breathe on a cold window. The patch made on the glass by your breath is wet. It is called **condensation**. If you touch the walls and windows of your kitchen or bathroom, you may find condensation there too.

9

Going up in a balloon

A layer of air surrounds the Earth like a huge cloud you cannot see. It is called the **atmosphere**. It starts at the ground where it is packed tight or **dense**. The atmosphere thins out to almost nothing at about 150 km (95 miles) above the Earth.

There is a force that pulls all this air, and everything else, towards the Earth. It is called **gravity**. If you hold a ball in your hand and let it drop, it falls to the ground because of gravity.

The first people to leave the ground and fly in the air lived 200 years ago. There were no airplanes then, and no engines. They had to overcome the force of gravity. They used hot air balloons. The rising force of the hot air lifted the balloons above the ground.

Balloons then and now

A hot air balloon rises because the hot air inside it is lighter than the cool air outside. Balloons are large bags. They are made of material through which air cannot pass. The first balloons were filled with hot air by holding them over fires.

The first hot air balloon was launched on June 4th, 1783 in France. It was built by Joseph and Etienne Montgolfier. These two brothers did not fly with their balloon.

The first man to go up in a balloon was another Frenchman, Jean de Rozier. He made his first flight on October 15th, 1783.

'A balloon can be made to go up and then come down when the pilot wants to land.'

Early balloons could make only short flights. Once they were flying, the hot air began to cool. There was no way of heating it up again. The hot air balloons of today fly long distances. They carry gas burners with them. More air can be heated by the burners during a flight.

Flying a balloon

Balloons have no engines. Once they are in the air, they are blown by the wind. The pilot is carried in a large basket underneath the balloon. If the balloon starts to lose height, the pilot burns more gas to make the air hotter. The basket carries bags of sand as **ballast**. When the sand is thrown out the balloon becomes lighter and floats upwards.

▲ Hot air balloons rising into the sky just after the start of a competition.

There is no way of steering a balloon. When the pilot wants to come down, he has to look ahead for a good place to land. He can make the balloon lose height by losing hot air. If the pilot does this with great care, the balloon will float down to land in the place he has chosen.

11

Water everywhere!

Without water, there would be no life on Earth. About three-quarters of the surface of the Earth is covered with water. There are five great oceans. There are rivers and lakes on the land. There is water in the air and under the ground.

Water always flows downhill to the sea. In most rivers, the water flows gently towards the sea. Sometimes the land slopes steeply. Then the water flows quickly through rapids, or pours over waterfalls.

Sea water

Sea water and fresh water are not the same. Sea water is full of **minerals** from the sea bed, and it is too salty to drink. The fresh water we drink comes from lakes, rivers and streams.

◀ See if you can find these falls in an atlas.
1. Angel Falls, Venezuela. 2. Victoria Falls, Zimbabwe.
3. Niagara Falls, USA/Canada.

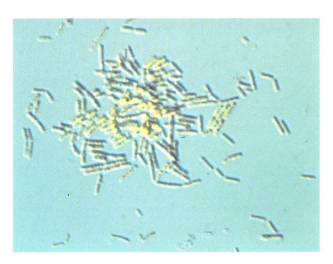

▲ This picture shows bacteria in a drop of water seen through a microscope.

The water we drink

Water in rivers and streams is not always safe to drink. Look at a drop of pond water under a **microscope**. You will see that water is not always as clean as it looks. Water sometimes contains harmful things. Some of these are tiny living things called **bacteria**. They can make you ill. In many parts of the world, the drinking water has to be boiled to kill the bacteria.

The purest water comes from wells and springs. It has trickled through sand and rocks which take out the harmful things. Some of this pure water is bottled for drinking. A gas called **carbon dioxide** can be added to still water to make it fizzy. The fizz is caused by gas bubbles escaping from the water when the bottle is shaken or opened.

Hard and soft water

Water that flows through chalky rocks picks up tiny pieces of chalk. It is fit to drink, but it is 'hard' water. If you use soap in hard water it does not make a good lather. It leaves a scum on the surface. Hard water can be made 'soft' by treating it in a water softener.

The softest water of all is rain water. This is soft because it has not had to flow through rocks.

soft water

hard water

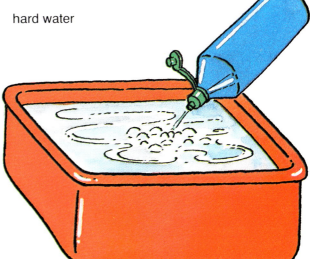

Floating and sinking

When you lie down in your bath, the level of the water rises. Your body takes the place of some of the water, or **displaces** it.

This happens when any solid object is placed in water. Some things sink. Others float. A cork floats. Part of it sticks up above the surface of the water. The cork displaces only a little water. A stone sinks to the bottom. It displaces more water than the cork. Heavy things displace more water than light things of the same size.

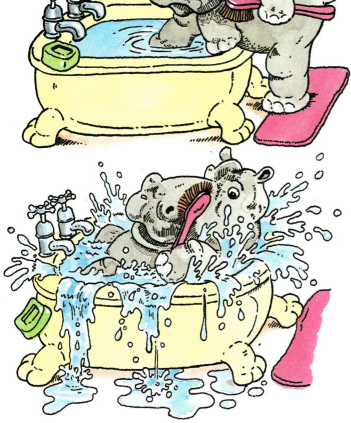

Rubber boats

Push a cork down below water and let it go. It will bob up and float on the surface. The reason that the cork floats is that it is lighter than the same amount of water. It has less **density**. The density of stone is greater than that of water. This is why the stone sinks.

The density of air is less than that of water. A rubber boat floats because it is filled with air. The greater the pressure of air inside it, the higher it floats on the water.

Floating

Not all water has the same density. The salt in sea water makes it more dense than fresh water. Objects float better in sea water. In some parts of the world, the water is very full of salt. Then it is easy for a person to float in the water. The Dead Sea, in the Middle East, is one of these places.

If you go sailing in a small boat, you have to wear a life-jacket. This has air in it. The air in your life-jacket will keep

▼ Floating in the Dead Sea is easy because the water is very full of salt.

▲ This picture shows a modern airship with New York skyscrapers in the background.

you afloat, if you fall into the water. The life-jacket is made so that you can keep your face above the water. This saves you from drowning.

Floating in air

When air is heated, it becomes less dense. This is why a balloon with hot air in it rises. It can float in the air.

Some gases are less dense than air. Helium is one of them. Modern airships have balloons filled with helium gas. An airship can be filled with enough gas to carry a heavy load of cargo and people. It can float in the air without sinking to the ground.

Working under water

Can you swim under water? Many people can. Most people can stay under for only a few seconds. They have to come up for air.

Some people may need to stay under water for quite a long time. They may want to explore wrecks or look at damaged ships. Many people like to study fish and rocks beneath the surface. They all need to have a supply of air.

Getting air is not the only problem. Water pressure is much greater than air pressure. The deeper a diver goes, the greater the pressure. Divers risk losing their lives if the pressure is too high.

▼ The diver on the left uses an air tank as he works under water. The one on the right is wearing a 'Big Jim' suit. Air is piped from a ship above.

Deep-sea diving

People who work under water often use diving suits. These are made of heavy rubber. They have strong helmets with thick glass windows. Air is pumped into a diving suit through a pipe from a ship on the surface. This air is the right pressure for the diver to withstand the pressure of the water.

A diver has to take great care when he comes back to the surface from deep down. One of the gases in air is called **nitrogen**. If divers come to the surface too fast, this gas stays in their bodies. It causes a sickness called the bends. Divers must come up slowly. That way they can breathe out most of the nitrogen first.

Scuba diving

Diving suits are clumsy to wear. Divers wearing these suits can only move slowly. Their lives depend on the air pipes linking them to the surface.

Other divers take their own supply of air with them. They carry metal air bottles on their backs. A tube leads from the bottles to a face-mask. The diver wears a rubber suit to keep warm. These divers are called scuba divers.

The air that scuba divers breathe is a mixture of oxygen and helium. There is little or no nitrogen in it. A scuba diver can come to the surface quickly without getting the bends.

Scuba divers can move about more easily than people in heavy diving suits can. Their gear is lighter, but they are less protected against water pressure. They cannot go deep or stay below so long as deep-sea divers can.

How does a submarine work?

A submarine is a ship built to move under water. It can dive beneath the water and come back to the surface. It can stay **submerged** for a long time.

Deep down in the sea the water pressure is very great. The submarine must be able to stand up to this pressure. Submarines have engines to drive them and rudders for steering. But other ships do not have to rise and fall in the water.

Buoyancy

Air is less dense than water. A rubber boat floats on the surface because of the air inside it. It is very **buoyant**. Submarines need to be buoyant beneath the surface as well.

A submarine has a number of large steel tanks along each side. When the tanks are filled with air, the submarine floats. If water is pumped into the tanks, it will sink, or submerge. For the ship to come to the surface again, water is blown out of the tanks. This is done by **compressed** air.

Staying submerged

It takes time to fill or empty the tanks. A submarine may need to dive or surface fast. It has hydroplanes to help with this. These are like the flaps on the wings of a plane. They can be moved up or down to help the submarine rise to the surface or dive.

A submarine can stay submerged for weeks or even months. It has its own air supply for the crew. It uses **radar** for finding the way. **Sonar** checks the depth of water beneath it.

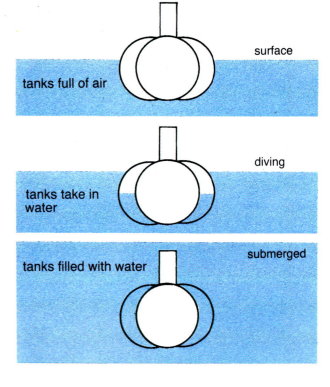

tanks full of air — surface

tanks take in water — diving

tanks filled with water — submerged

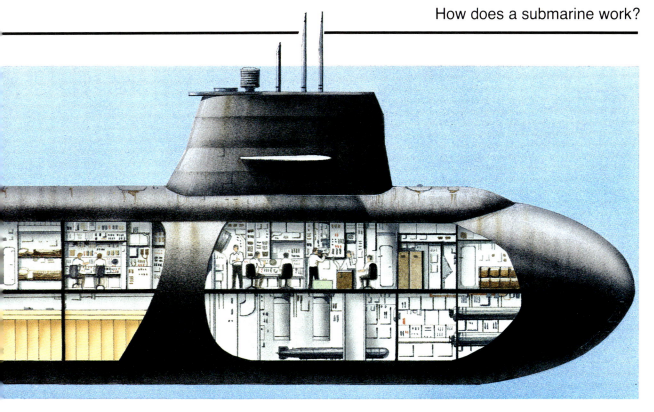

Understanding ice

Ice is water which has frozen solid. Water freezes when the heat of the water falls to 0 degrees centigrade (32 degrees Fahrenheit). If the heat rises to above 0°C (32°F), the ice turns back into water.

Ice is less dense than water, so it floats. It floats low down because it is not much lighter than water. Float a cube of ice in water and see for yourself. There is more ice beneath the water than there is above it.

What are icebergs?

The seas in the Arctic and around Antarctica are frozen into ice. In warmer weather, pieces of ice break off. They are called **icebergs**, and float around in the sea. The largest iceberg ever seen was 335 km (208 miles) long.

Ice floats low in the water. So most of an iceberg is hidden under the surface. This is why icebergs are a great danger to ships. Ice under the water is as dangerous as rock.

If all the ice at the Poles were to melt, the level of the sea would rise all over the world. You can find out for yourself how this would happen.

Put some water and a lot of ice-cubes in a large plastic bowl. Now put in a stone big enough to stick up above the water. Mark the water level with a pencil. Wait for the ice to melt. What happens to the water level?

▼ The iceberg in the picture looks like a huge block of ice cream. There is much more under the water.

Moving on ice

After a long journey, the tires of a car are warm. Rubbing on the road makes them hot. When a car travels on ice, the heat of the tires melts the surface. This forms a thin layer of water. The road becomes slippery. Drivers have to go slow on ice to make sure that their cars do not skid. It is hard to steer a car that is skidding. It is also difficult to stop on ice. This is what makes icy roads very dangerous.

We can, however, make use of slippery ice when we take part in winter sports. The blades of skates work like the car tires. They melt the surface so that the skates can slide over the ice.

Toboggans and bobsleds have smooth runners that work in the same way. A toboggan like the one in the picture can travel downhill at a speed of more than 80 kph (50 mph).

film of water   ice

Steam and water power

Water boils at 100°C (212°F). At this heat, water changes into **steam**. Steam takes up a lot more space than water.

When water boils in a pan or a kettle, steam rushes to escape. You can see the jet of steam when you watch a kettle boiling. A jet of steam can be turned into power to drive things. The first railway engines were driven by steam power.

Water power

Cold water can also be used to drive things. It can be used at a **hydroelectric** power station to make electricity. These stations are found where there is plenty of water from rivers or mountains. The water is stored in huge lakes called **reservoirs**. Dams are built to hold the water back.

The water pours down a pipe by the force of gravity. At the end of the pipe, the water rushes out as a very powerful jet. This jet of water drives the blades of a wheel called a **turbine**. The turbine turns very fast and makes electricity. The water goes on to join a river below the power station.

▲ This shows how a hydroelectric turbine works. Water pours down a pipe from a huge dam. The water spins the blades of the turbine as it rushes past. The shaft drives another turbine to make electricity.

A steam turbine

A steam turbine works like a turbine driven by water. It is made of several wheels and hundreds of blades.

Water is boiled by burning coal, oil or gas. This makes steam. The steam is passed through pipes to the turbine. As the steam hits the blades of the turbine, it makes them turn. The turbine can then make electricity.

Steam turbines are used in most power stations. They are also used to make power for ships.

The power of waves and tides

The fuels used to run power stations are very expensive. One day, some of these fuels, such as oil and gas, may run out. There is plenty of water, however, and water is free.

▲ This enormous steam turbine produces electricity in a power station. The covers have been taken off for the turbine to be inspected. Note the rows of blades.

One kind of water power is used very little. It is the sea. If you have been by the sea on a windy day, you will have seen the power of the waves.

Only a few power stations in the world use waves and tides to make electricity. The world's first tidal power station is at the Rance river in France. One day, there may be many more power stations like this one. Then the world would not need so much oil and coal.

How are winds caused?

Air is on the move all the time. When air moves from one place to another, it makes a wind. Sometimes the wind is just a gentle breeze that you can feel on your face. At other times, the wind becomes a gale and can blow down trees.

Pressure

The pressure of air in the atmosphere is different in different places. When the air is cold, it is heavy. It presses down on the Earth to make an area of high pressure. The heat of the Sun warms the cold air. It becomes lighter and rises. This makes an area of low pressure.

As warm air rises, cold air rushes in to take its place. Air moves from an area of high pressure to one of low pressure. This is how winds are caused.

HIGH

LOW

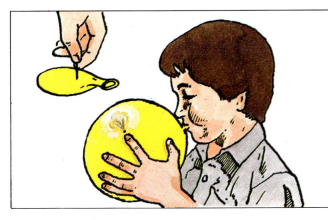

You can see for yourself how this works. Make a small pinhole in a balloon, then blow it up. Now put your finger close to the hole. You will feel the air rushing out. The air is moving from the high pressure area inside the balloon to the low pressure area outside. You have made a wind!

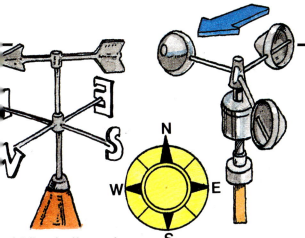

The Beaufort wind scale is used to describe the kind of wind, and its force at different speeds. For example, Force 8 is a gale. It blows at a speed of 61 to 75 kph (37 to 46 mph). A gale can do a lot of damage.

Wind direction

Winds blow in all directions. We need to know which way the winds are blowing. This helps us to know what kind of weather to expect.

We name winds by the direction they are blowing from. A north wind blows from north to south. An east wind blows from east to west. A weather vane is an instrument which shows the way the wind is blowing. Its four arms point north, south, east and west. The vane catches the wind. It swings around to show where the wind is coming from.

The speed of the wind

Strong winds are a danger to ships at sea. They can damage buildings and flatten crops in the fields. Weather **forecasts** on the radio or television give the speed of the wind as well as its direction. Sometimes you may hear a gale warning.

Weather forecasters use an **anemometer** to measure the speed of the wind. This has cups set to catch the wind as it blows. They are fixed to a metal rod. As the wind blows into the cups, the rod turns. The number of turns can be shown on a dial to give the speed.

Using wind

▲ Gliders use thermals to gain height.

Before ships had engines, all large ships used sails to keep them moving. If there was no wind, ships would just drift. A ship might take days to travel just a few miles. Sailors knew that there were some parts of the oceans which were often calm. The crew could run out of food and water.

The best winds for the sailing ships of those days were the trade winds. These were steady winds that blew in the same direction all the year round. They blew towards the Equator from east to west. Further north and also to the south were the Westerlies. These winds blew from west to east. Ships that used these winds were able to keep up a good speed.

Riding on air

Glider pilots make use of air **currents**. Currents of rising warm air are called **thermals**. They help gliders to fly higher and stay in the air longer. A skilled pilot knows where to find thermals. Warm air rises above the slopes near open country. It rises, too, over cliff tops and masses of rocks.

Using wind for fun

People all over the world take part in sports which use the wind. People who sail in small boats get fun out of using the wind. They have to learn to sail against the wind, and to tack. This means moving the sail from side to side. Then the boat moves forward on a zig-zag course.

Windsurfing is another popular sport. It is done on a surf-board fitted with a sail. The windsurfer holds on to bars which are fixed to the sail. The windsurfer is able to move the sail around, so as to make use of the wind.

▲ This is a modern windmill. Can you describe how it is different from an old windmill?

Modern windmills

For hundreds of years, people used windmills to grind their corn. Today, in some parts of the world, modern wind-mills are used to make electricity. They are called wind turbines. Their sails are made of light metal and are shaped like airplane propellers. The wind turns the sails to make electricity. Wind turbines only work well in places where there is plenty of wind all the time.

Wind and water

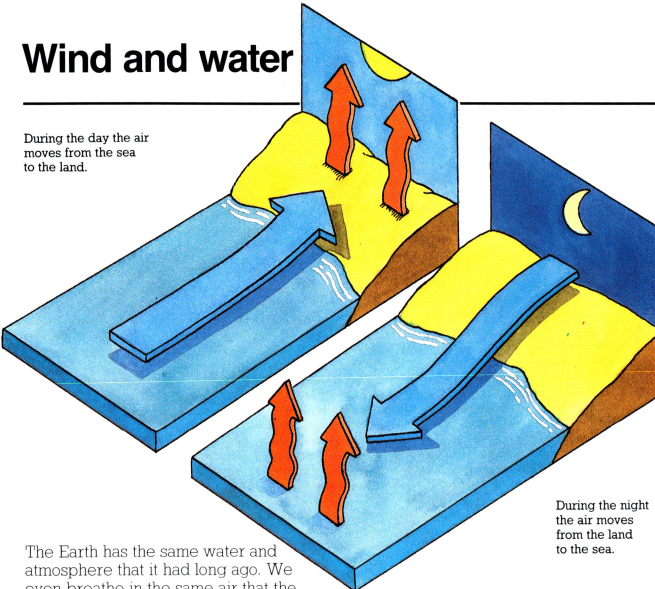

During the day the air moves from the sea to the land.

During the night the air moves from the land to the sea.

The Earth has the same water and atmosphere that it had long ago. We even breathe in the same air that the dinosaurs once breathed. None of the Earth's air and water is ever lost or destroyed. Plants and animals need air and water to stay alive.

Wind and water are **circulating** or moving across the Earth all the time. They act together to give us our changing weather. They bring rain to the land so that we can grow crops.

Land and sea breezes

When the Sun shines, it warms up the land and the sea. The land heats up and cools down faster than the sea. Warm air rises over the land. Cool air comes in from the sea to take its place. This is why there are sea breezes at the coast.

The land cools when the Sun goes down. Warm air continues to rise from the sea. Cool air moves from the land to take its place. This causes land or offshore breezes in the evening.

All this takes place in one day. A similar **cycle** of wind happens through the year. The land warms up in the summer months. This makes winds blow from the sea. It cools in the winter. Now cold winds blow away from the land.

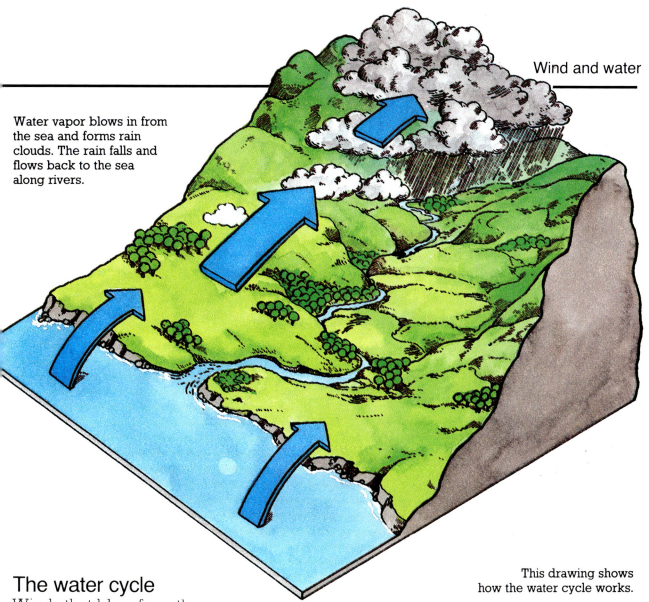

Water vapor blows in from the sea and forms rain clouds. The rain falls and flows back to the sea along rivers.

This drawing shows how the water cycle works.

The water cycle

Winds that blow from the sea carry water vapor. This vapor rises to form clouds. When the clouds cool down, this vapor **condenses** to form drops of water. These water drops fall as rain.

The rain trickles through the soil. It flows into the rivers and streams, and in time goes back to the sea. There, each drop of water is ready to start the water cycle all over again.

Rain is needed to give us drinking water and to help grow crops. In many parts of the world, people know when to expect rain. They plant their crops to fit in with the rainfall pattern. They know when to expect the sunshine that will ripen the crops and the fruit. These people are lucky. They have a **stable** climate throughout the year.

People who live in some lands are not so lucky. Their climate is not so stable. If the rains do not come, their crops will fail. When this happens, many people may starve. Then they need help from the rest of the world.

29

Rain and snow

polar regions

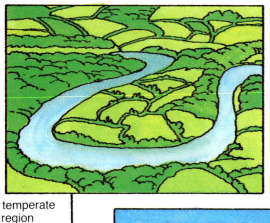

temperate region

desert

There are many different climates in the world. At the North and South Poles it is very cold all the year round. In parts of the desert lands of Africa and Asia, hardly any rain falls. In the forests near the Equator, it rains for weeks on end.

In other places, the weather is different at each of the seasons of the year. It is cold in winter and warm in summer. In the spring and autumn there is often more wind and rain. It is more pleasant to live in places where the climate is **temperate**. This is because it is not too hot, not too cold, not too wet and not too dry. Most of the United States and most of Europe have temperate climates.

Why rain falls

When the Sun shines on the ocean it warms the sea and the air above it. Tiny drops of moisture rise up from the sea as water vapor. This vapor is carried up with the warm air as it rises. This is called **evaporation**. After a shower of rain, you can see vapor rising above a puddle as the Sun shines on it. The puddle steams in the heat.

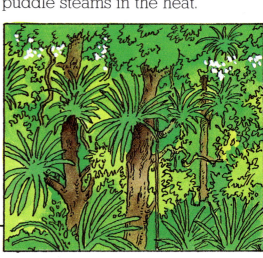

rain forest

If there is not much wind, the vapor in the air may condense near to the ground. Then it forms mist or fog. In cities, where there is dust in the air, the fog picks up the dust. This makes a thick, dirty fog which is called 'smog'.

Vapor that rises high in the air forms clouds. When the clouds cool, the moisture in them condenses into larger drops of water. These drops fall as rain or snow.

Rain, sleet and snow

Rain often falls through very cold air before it reaches the ground. Then it becomes sleet or snow. Near the North and South Poles the air is always cold. There, rain always turns to snow before it reaches the ground. There are other parts of the world where the air is never cold enough for snow. People living there never see snow.

Hail is formed from raindrops. These spin around in cold air as they fall to the ground. Layers of ice form on them as they fall.

On high mountains the air is always cold. Snow becomes hard and turns into ice. Great slabs of ice slide down mountain valleys to form **glaciers**. You can think of these as rivers of ice.

Climbing a mountain

Mountain climbing is a dangerous sport. People who do this have great skill. They need to be very fit. They must make careful plans before the climb begins. The climbers must know what weather to expect, and what equipment they will need to take.

On high mountains, the air is cold and less dense. Above 4000 meters (13,122 feet), it is difficult to breathe. The climbers take oxygen with them. This makes it easier to breathe and to work.

Base camp

The team first sets up a base camp at the foot of the mountain. This is where they keep stores and equipment. They need nylon ropes, ice axes and other climbing tools. The climb will take several days. On the way, they will have to set up a camp each night.

Attack on the summit

The first part of the climb is the easiest. The climbers reach the point where the trees stop. This is called the **treeline**. Then they reach snow at the snowline. They rest at a camp near the snowline before they begin the final climb to the summit.

Now the real climbing starts. It becomes harder to breathe. Every movement is more tiring. The climbers wear goggles to protect their eyes from the bright light. There is a risk of becoming snowblind without goggles. The air is very cold and there is the danger of frostbite.

Soon the climb becomes really dangerous. The climbers are roped together in case one of them falls. They may have to cross glaciers, using ice picks. They climb along steep rock walls by **traversing**. Each step they take may start a landslide, or an avalanche of falling snow. In one of these, a huge amount of snow may fall, burying one or other of the climbers.

As they near the top, they climb more slowly. They watch out for bad weather. A **blizzard** of icy cold driving snow could make them stop or turn back. But they are nearly there. At last, they climb the final rock face and reach the summit. The climbers have challenged the mountain, and won!

◀ 1. Pitons (iron pegs) 2. Goggles 3. Climbing helmet 4. Climbing boots 5. Nylon rope 6. Ice axe

summit

route
taken by
climbers

treeline

base camp

Research Library
AIMS Education Foundation
Fresno, CA 93747-8120

33

Stormy weather

In most parts of the world, there is a pattern to the climate. Farmers know when it is likely to be cold, hot, wet or dry. They sow their crops when rain is expected. The seeds need rain to grow. Then the Sun comes to ripen the harvest. If rain and Sun do not come at the right time, the crop may be spoilt.

▼ Trying to keep dry during the monsoon rains.

The monsoon

Some parts of Asia have a monsoon climate. There are two seasons in the year. One is hot and dry, the other is hot and wet. Monsoon winds blow from a different direction in each season.

In the hot dry summer, the land heats up. Soon the monsoon blows in from the sea and brings heavy rain. The rains start suddenly. Rain may fall for months without stopping. Then it causes floods. In winter, the land cools down. Dry winds blow from the land towards the sea.

In some years the monsoon fails or comes too late. Then the harvest is poor and thousands of people do not have enough to eat.

▼ In summer, wet winds blow off the Indian Ocean.

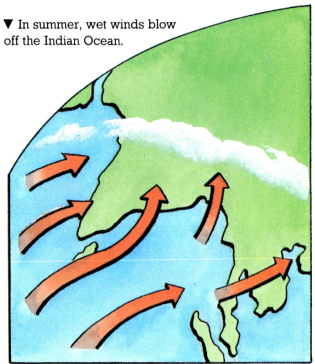

▼ In winter, dry winds blow off the land.

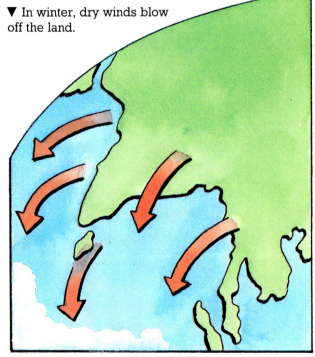

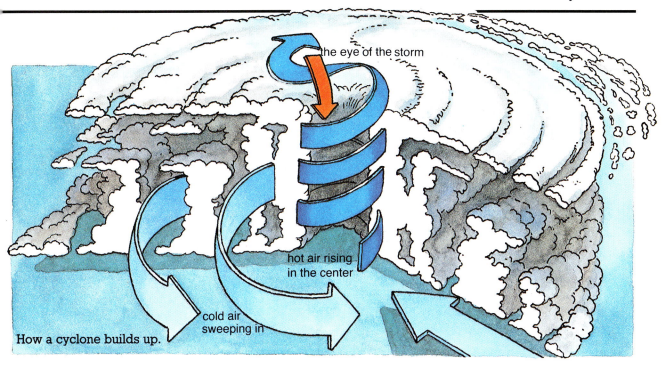

the eye of the storm

hot air rising
in the center

cold air
sweeping in

How a cyclone builds up.

Cyclones

Hurricanes or **cyclones** are very fierce storms. In the Far East they are called typhoons. They start in mid-ocean near the Equator.

Hot, moist air rises over a large area of ocean. This air begins to move in a spiral pattern, as in the picture. It does this because the Earth is spinning. An area of very low pressure is formed. Cooler winds sweep in towards the center at very great speed. At the center of the cyclone is an area where there is no wind. It is called the eye of the storm.

Most cyclones die out over the sea. If they reach land, then winds of 150 kph (93 mph) or more can do great damage.

When cool air falls over a large area, it forms an **anticyclone**. This is an area of high pressure. Here the winds move away from the center.

Tornadoes

A **tornado** or 'twister' is a violent column of wind shaped like a funnel. It twists at very high speed over a very small area. A tornado can sweep over the ground at speeds of up to 80 kph (50 mph). It can destroy trees and buildings in its path.

Thunderstorms

The electricity we use to light our homes travels along wires. It is called current electricity. There is another kind called **static**. Static electricity stays in one place. It builds up in some things as a **charge** of electricity. It stays there until it is **discharged**.

▶ Comb your hair very quickly for 30 seconds. Then hold the comb just above your hair and see what happens.

Sometimes, when you comb your hair in the dark, strange things happen. Your hair crackles, and you may see sparks. The charge of static in your hair is discharged into the comb. This is caused by the rubbing action of the comb, called **friction**.

Thunder and lightning are due to static electricity, but on a huge scale.

A thundercloud

You may have seen a thundercloud rising high into the sky. Inside the cloud there are very strong air currents. The cloud is also full of moisture.

As moist air rises in the strong currents, water droplets and hail are formed. They rub against each other causing friction. After a time, large charges of static build up in the cloud. There is one charge near the top, where tiny drops of ice collect. The bottom of the cloud, which is full of rain, is also full of static. When a cloud has too much static, a thunderstorm begins.

Thunder and lightning

In a thunderstorm, static is discharged. This produces the huge sparks we know as lightning. These may flash and flicker from one part of the cloud to the other. They also pass from one cloud to another cloud. The whole sky is lit up with flashes. This is called sheet lightning.

It is called forked lightning when it discharges from the cloud to the ground. The 'fork' finds the easiest way to Earth. This is often to a tall tree or to a high building, such as a church.

The air expands when it is heated by the immense heat of the lightning. This makes the crack of thunder. Thunder and lightning both happen at the same time. You see the lightning first because light travels faster than sound.

The speed of sound

You can see a flash of lightning at almost the second it takes place. The sound of thunder comes later. Count the seconds between the flash and the thunder. It takes the sound about 3 seconds to travel 1 km (0.6 miles) between you and the storm. If you count up to 30 seconds, the storm is about 10 km (6 miles) away.

Sound can travel at 1200 kph (750 mph). Light travels at 300,000 kilometers per second (186,000 miles per second).

▲ Is this sheet or forked lightning?

Looking at weather maps

A weather forecast tells us what the weather will be like in the next day or two. You may need to know this if you are planning a trip, or going on holiday. Many people, such as farmers, need to know because of their work.

Forecasters measure the pressure of the atmosphere, using an instrument called a barometer. They find out if it is going to be low or high. From this, they build up a weather picture on a map. Pressure is measured in **millibars**. Normal pressure is 1000 millibars. Readings below this show low pressure. Readings above show high pressure.

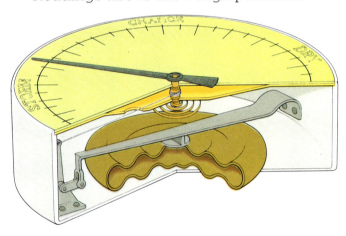

▲ This is called an aneroid barometer. Pressure is measured by the amount by which air squashes the inside box, colored light brown in the illustration. This makes the pointer move on the dial.

Lows and highs

Lines on a weather map link all the places with the same pressure. They show high and low pressure areas. Lows are cyclones, and they bring wet weather. Highs are anticyclones. They bring good, settled weather.

Forecasters study the way that lows and highs are moving. By doing this, they can say what kind of weather is on the way.

▼ What is the lowest pressure shown in this part of a weather map?

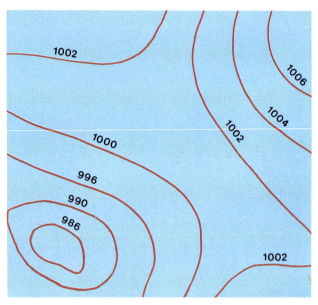

Cold and warm fronts

Other lines on weather maps show warm or cold **fronts**. A front is the dividing line between cold air and warm air. Fronts are formed when warm and cold air meet each other.

When cold air moves towards warm air, it pushes in beneath it. The warm air rises, and moisture condenses. Then thunderclouds build up and there may be a storm. This is a cold front.

When warm air meets cold air, it rises slowly above the cold air. This makes a warm front. The moisture in the warm air condenses and forms clouds. These clouds will bring rain.

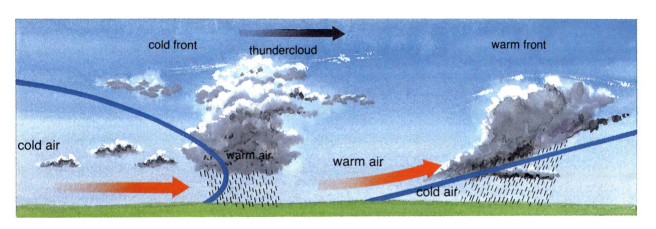

cold front

thundercloud

warm front

cold air

warm air

warm air

cold air

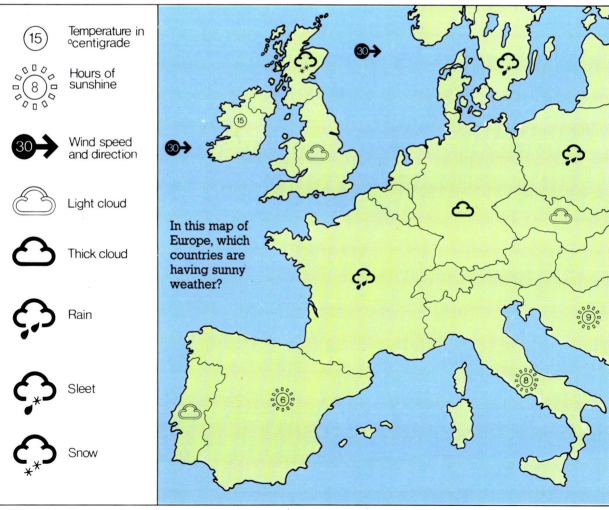

(15) Temperature in °centigrade

(8) Hours of sunshine

30➡ Wind speed and direction

Light cloud

Thick cloud

Rain

Sleet

Snow

In this map of Europe, which countries are having sunny weather?

Weather satellites

Weather reports tell us what the weather is now. From these we can forecast what it will be like in the future. To do this we need to have reports from the places where our weather comes from.

These used to be sent by weather stations on land, and by weather ships at sea. Now **satellites** in space have made weather forecasts easier. They can give a clear picture of the weather all over the land and sea. They help the weathermen to make more accurate forecasts.

How does a satellite see?

Each satellite moves around the Earth in **orbit**. There are cameras on board that keep taking pictures. These are sent back to Earth. The pictures are put together to make large weather maps. As well as clouds, they show snow cover and floating pack ice. They can be made larger to show up small details.

Satellites can also take pictures at night. These pictures show warm and cold areas in different colours. These also help the weathermen.

▼ A tracking station on the ground picks up the signals from the satellite in space.

Keeping in touch

How do these pictures reach the Earth? The satellite takes still pictures. These are stored on tape. On the Earth, below the satellite, there are **tracking stations**. You can see one in the picture.

When the satellite passes overhead, it sends the tracking station pictures by radio signals. These are passed to a weather center. There the signals are changed into pictures we can see.

▼ The three pictures, taken by a satellite at different times, show bad weather moving towards the British Isles from the Atlantic Ocean.

Changing weather

Pictures taken over the same area in a number of orbits can be looked at. They show how weather patterns change and move.

The weathermen on the ground can see how clouds are building up along warm and cold fronts. They can see the swirl of cloud as a cyclone grows. They can watch a storm build up far out at sea. The weathermen can give us all warnings of frost and snow, gales and hurricanes. Most people want to be warned about these things.

Looking after water

▲ Water being used to irrigate crops.

All plants and animals need water. In some parts of the world there is more than is needed. In others, there is not enough water. Water is often allowed to become **polluted** with oil or waste from cities. Then it is unfit to drink or to support life. Sometimes water which could be stored is allowed to flow away unused.

Millions of gallons of water are used each day in a large city. This water is stored in reservoirs. These are made by flooding river valleys. Dams are built across the valleys to keep the water back.

Irrigation

Water is needed for growing crops. Rain water can be stored and used for crops in the dry season. This is called **irrigation**. One way is to cut channels from a river or reservoir. The water flows along the channels into the fields. Sometimes the water is carried along pipes to sprinklers. These spray water over the growing plants.

In some parts of the world, like India, there is only one wet season. Here a second crop can be grown in the same year by making use of irrigation.

Keeping water clean

Water for drinking must be pure and clean. Water comes to your home from a waterworks. Here water is **filtered** in sand beds. The water trickles slowly through the sand. The sand takes out the dirt and bacteria.

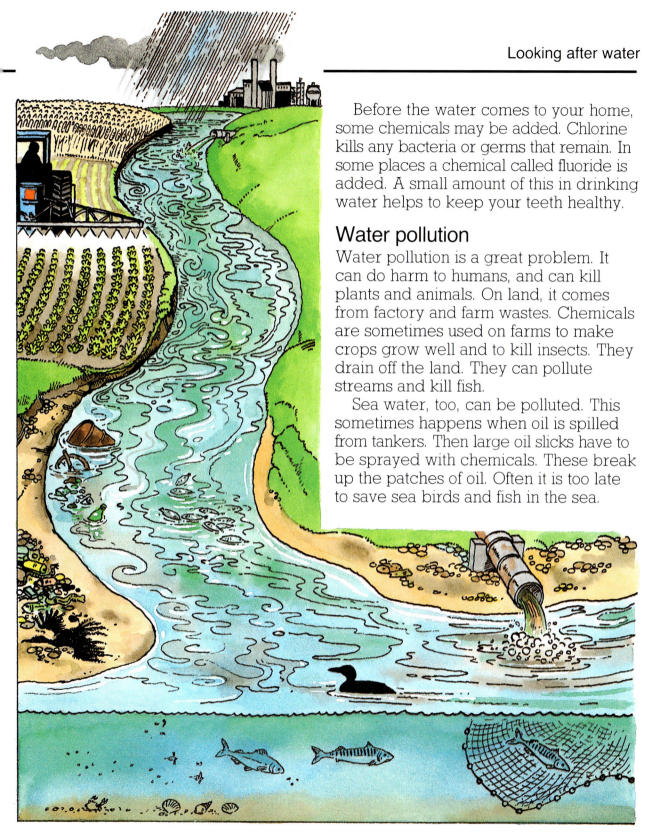

Before the water comes to your home, some chemicals may be added. Chlorine kills any bacteria or germs that remain. In some places a chemical called fluoride is added. A small amount of this in drinking water helps to keep your teeth healthy.

Water pollution

Water pollution is a great problem. It can do harm to humans, and can kill plants and animals. On land, it comes from factory and farm wastes. Chemicals are sometimes used on farms to make crops grow well and to kill insects. They drain off the land. They can pollute streams and kill fish.

Sea water, too, can be polluted. This sometimes happens when oil is spilled from tankers. Then large oil slicks have to be sprayed with chemicals. These break up the patches of oil. Often it is too late to save sea birds and fish in the sea.

Clean air

We need clean air to keep healthy. Air, like water, can be polluted. In cities, fumes from cars and trucks make us cough and choke. Smoke pours into the air from factories and power stations. Sometimes accidents at factories can send poisons into the air. This happened in 1984 at Bhopal, in India. Thousands of people died.

Even in the country the air is not always clean. Crops are often sprayed with chemicals from the air. This can harm animal life if it is not done carefully.

Radiation is another kind of air pollution. You cannot see it or smell it, but it can cause sickness and death. It can pass into the air from accidents at nuclear power stations. This happened at Chernobyl, in the USSR, in 1986.

Not all pollution kills plants or animals, but it makes them less healthy. In cities, it can attack the brick and stone of buildings and eat it away. We have to look after our air and keep it clean. All life depends upon it. Dirty air is a threat to all living things.

Glossary

anemometer: an instrument used for measuring the speed of the wind

anticyclone: a large area of high pressure from which winds blow outwards. As the anticyclone moves, it brings settled weather in the area covered

atmosphere: the mass of air that surrounds the Earth

bacteria: minute living things, some of which may cause disease

ballast: heavy material, such as sand

blizzard: a storm of wind and snow

buoyant: able to float

carbon dioxide: one of the gases in air. It is made up of carbon and oxygen. It has no color or smell

charge: to fill with electricity. An amount of electricity held in something

circulate: to keep moving around in the same space

climate: the usual weather in a part of the world throughout the year

compress: to squeeze together. A gas can be compresed

condensation: the liquid formed when a gas is cooled and turned into a liquid

condense: to change a gas into a liquid by cooling it. A liquid takes up less space than a gas

convection: the movement of heat in a liquid or gas. The hot liquid or gas rises to the top and the cold sinks

current: a flow of water, air or electricity

cycle: a chain of events that take place in the same order, over and over again

cyclone: a large area of low pressure with winds blowing towards the center. It is usually called a depression

dense: describes something where the parts or material are packed close together

density: the amount of material in something compared with the space it takes up

discharge: to give up an electric charge

displace: to take the place of something. A ship displaces an amount of water

evaporation: changing a liquid into a vapor by heating it

expansion: the process of getting larger and taking up more space

filter: to separate something solid from a liquid

force: energy, power or strength. A force cannot be seen

forecast: to say what will happen in the future. A statement about the future

friction: the force that slows down movement and produces heat

front: a line along which one mass of air meets another mass which is hotter or colder

gas: one of the three states of matter. The other two are solids and liquids. Gases have no shape. Air is a mixture of gases

glacier: a slow-moving river of ice

gravity: a force we cannot see. Gravity gives people and objects weight

helium: a very light gas, lighter than air

hydroelectric: producing electricity from the energy of moving water

hydrogen: a gas that is lighter than air. It is the lightest gas and burns easily

iceberg: a large mass of ice that has broken off from a larger one and floats in the sea

irrigation: watering land or crops by using channels or pipes

liquid: one of the three states of matter. The other two are gases and solids. Liquids flow, but not so easily as gases do

microscope: an instrument you can use to make very small objects appear larger

millibar: a unit used for measuring the pressure of the atmosphere. The normal pressure is equal to 1000 millibars

mineral: any natural material found in the ground. Iron, salt and stone are minerals

moisture: dampness; water that is present in the air as water vapor or mist

nitrogen: a gas with no smell, color or taste. It makes up a large part of air

orbit: the path of a satellite as it moves around another object in space. The Moon is in orbit around the Earth

HIEBERT LIBRARY

3 6877 00224 0330

Glossary

oxygen: a gas that is a part of air and water. Oxygen has no color, taste or smell. We need it to stay alive

planet: any one of the bodies in space that revolves around the Sun. The Earth is a planet, so is Mars

pollute: to spoil and put poison into the atmosphere, the land and water

pressure: a pushing or squeezing force. The pressure of the atmosphere presses on every part of the Earth's surface

radar: radar is short for **ra**dio **d**etecting **a**nd **r**anging. Radio waves are bounced off an object. The return is timed to work out how far away the object is

reservoir: a large tank or lake where water is stored

satellite: a body in orbit around a larger body in space. The Moon is a satellite of the Earth

solid: any material that is not a liquid or a gas. A solid has a definite shape and volume

sonar: sonar is short for **so**und, **n**avigation **a**nd **r**anging. Sonar is used by ships to measure how deep the water is

stable: steady, tending to stay the same

static: an electric charge that builds up on something until it is discharged. Static is caused by friction

steam: water vapor that you cannot see. It is produced by boiling water

submerge: to sink beneath the water or to put something beneath water

temperate: neither very hot, nor very cold

thermal: warm air rising above the ground. Thermals are used by glider pilots to help them gain height

tornado: a violent wind storm that moves across a small strip of land at a high speed

tracking station: a ground station from which the positions of earth satellites are tracked

traverse: to move across a rock face when climbing a mountain

treeline: the line on the side of a mountain above which trees cannot grow because it is too cold for them

turbine: a shaft to which a number of curved blades are fixed. The turbine is made to turn at high speed by a gas or water. Turbines are used to drive ships' propellers, and to make electricity in power stations

water vapor: water in the form of a gas. There is always some water vapor in air

DATE DUE

12/15/15			